A van came to the house.

1

"What a big van!" said Chip.

"What a big man!" said Kipper.

The man looked at the things.

"What a lot of things!" he said.

Mum and Dad helped the man.
They put things in the van.

"What a job!" said Dad.

The children helped too. Kipper
put his toys in the van.

Biff and Chip put the
go-kart in.

They put a box in the van.
"What a big box!" said Biff.

"What a job!" said everyone.

"Goodbye," said Biff.
"Goodbye," said Chip.

"Come and play soon," they said.

The van went to the new house.

Dad looked at Biff and Chip.
"Oh no!" said Biff and Chip.

"What a job!" they said.